Famous
SAXOPHONE
SOLOS

from R&B, Pop, and Smooth Jazz

Jeff Harrington

Edited by Jonathan Feist

D0584827

Berklee Press

Vice President: David Kusek
Dean of Continuing Education: Debbie Cavalier
Chief Operating Officer: Robert F. Green
Managing Editor: Jonathan Feist
Editorial Assistants: Yousun Choi, Martin Fowler, Amy Kaminski, Jacqueline Sim
Cover Design: Betty Foley (bfoleydesign.com)

Transcribed by Jeff Harrington

ISBN 978-0-87639-112-9

DISTRIBUTED BY

HAL•LEONARD®

1140 Boylston Street
Boston, MA 02215-3693 USA
(617) 747-2146

Visit Berklee Press Online at
www.berkleepress.com

7777 W. BLUEMOUND RD. P.O. BOX 13819
MILWAUKEE, WISCONSIN 53213

Visit Hal Leonard Online at
www.halleonard.com

Copyright © 2010 Berklee Press
All Rights Reserved

No part of this publication may be reproduced in any form or by
any means without the prior written permission of the Publisher.

CONTENTS

How to Work on Solo Transcriptions

Working on solo transcriptions is one of the most important and effective ways to master any style of improvised music. By playing, listening to, analyzing, and ultimately memorizing solos by great players, we are learning directly from the masters, absorbing all of their nuances of style, technique, phrasing, inflections, and vocabulary.

SUGGESTIONS FOR PRACTICING

The first thing to do is to obtain the original recording. Listen repeatedly to it while looking at the transcription. Notice any nuances of inflection and rhythm. For example, listen for ghost notes (indicated on the transcription by an "x" for the notehead). Notice any bending or glissandos as well as changes in dynamics and tone. Try to hear and play the articulation (slurring and tonguing combinations) exactly as on the recording. All of this can be quite challenging, requiring repeated and intense listening. Also, notice if the soloist is *interpreting the time* by playing behind the beat or on top, pushing the feel. This is a common technique that is relatively easy to hear but impractical to notate.

During the process of learning the solo, frequently go back and listen to the recording. It will actually make playing it much easier. Hearing the recording is an effortless way to instantly grasp many aspects of the solo. Without realizing it, a wealth of information comes to us simply by listening.

DIFFICULT PASSAGES

Treat the transcription just like you would any other written piece of music. That is, work to perfect all manner of technique, tone, rhythm, and phrasing. Begin familiarizing yourself with the piece by reading through it. The first goal should naturally be to accurately play the notes and rhythms. In the beginning, practice the transcription slowly with a metronome, gradually increasing your speed over time until you finally arrive at the recorded tempo. Slowing down the original recording and playing along can be helpful, but make sure you are playing the rhythms exactly and not just approximating them. Learning a solo can take weeks—even months—to master.

As you are working on the solo, identify difficult passages and begin breaking them down into smaller phrases to be worked over and repeated, first slowly, and then gradually faster. Once the piece is familiar, concentrate on these tricky areas rather than simply playing the piece over and over from start to finish. Breaking down the solo by focusing your efforts on the challenging sections will speed up your overall progress. Once you've worked out the tough spots, go back and read through the entire solo with a metronome set at a modest tempo geared to playing the difficult passages.

Remember, it is always better to play under tempo and technically accurately than to play too fast and thus sloppily with mistakes of notes or rhythm. No tempo is too slow! This way, you are building a foundation for your technique slowly and gradually. Once you find that tempo at which you can play the entire piece, try moving the metronome up two degrees faster. If you are successful at the new tempo, move it up another two notches. Keep doing this until you can no longer play the piece without mistakes. At that point, go back and work on the passages that are holding you back.

When you have attained an acceptable level of proficiency, you should play along with the original recording. By using transcribing software such as Transcriber or The Amazing Slow Downer, the tempo can be slowed down if the original is still too fast.

DIFFICULT RHYTHMS

A simple practice technique for understanding, counting, and ultimately *feeling* complex rhythmic passages is to play or sing the rhythm on one pitch. If the rhythm includes ties, then first practice without and then with the ties. Subdividing the rhythms this way will help you to *feel* them more accurately.

IMITATING STYLE

The ultimate goal, of course, is to be able to play the solo and have it sound exactly like the original. Replicating someone's style can take a long time, but it's a great endeavor, as it expands on and helps to develop and deepen our own style. Once you have perfected the technical aspects, a good approach to copying the stylistic elements is to listen to only a short phrase. Then play it, incorporating all the various nuances of inflection and articulation. Then listen and play again. Each time, you should both notice more details and get closer to the original. When practicing, always remember to take your time. The reward for quality and patient work is steady growth and progress.

MEMORIZE A PHRASE, SEVERAL CHORUSES, OR THE ENTIRE SOLO

After you have gotten fairly far in the process of learning the solo (even if you're under tempo), think about committing some or all of it to memory. This is especially important if you want it to seep into your own improvisation. Practice memorizing one phrase at a time. It is often helpful to first sing the phrase and then try to play it. Try to sing the exact pitches and intervals—slowly. Of course, it's not realistic to sing fast sixteenth-note passages unless they are done very slowly with all pitches clear and precise. Practicing singing the solo is an excellent way to internalize the music. It is much more likely to influence your own improvisation if you can sing it. Also, read the phrase and then try playing it without looking, glancing back if you can't remember.

By repeating these approaches and also by simply playing the piece many times, you will eventually memorize it. Make sure to memorize not just the notes but also the rhythms, and don't forget, the rests must be exact, too. At first, however, when memorizing, you don't need to adhere to a strict tempo overall. Go slowly to give yourself time to "hear" and remember what comes next.

ANALYZE THE MELODIC CONTENT, HARMONY, RHYTHM, AND PHRASING

A lot can be learned by analyzing the content of a transcription. Of course, the ability to do this depends on the extent of one's theoretical knowledge. It might be necessary to study more jazz theory to take full advantage of this approach. When analyzing the harmony, first analyze the chord progression and overall form of the tune. It might be blues changes, a standard with a lot of II V I progressions, or a pop progression. The form could be AABA, 12-bar blues, etc. Then analyze each note with regards to the chord being played at the time. Write numbers beneath each note thus identifying its function. For example, a note might be the 5th of the chord, or the ♯9, or a chromatic passing tone, etc. This way, you can get an overall idea of how the lines are constructed and what kind of harmonic vocabulary is being used. Eventually, you can incorporate this knowledge into your own playing. Additionally, when you play or listen to the solo, you will learn to associate the "sound" of the line with the actual harmony. If the solo uses a ♯11 on a major 7 chord, for instance, you will, after analyzing it, begin to identify that sound. When you hear it again in a different context, you will recognize it as a ♯11. You will also be more likely to utilize it in your own playing.

You can also look for melodic structure. For example, are there sequences or patterns? Is there thematic development? Are the intervals wide or close? Another area to look at is rhythm. What kinds of rhythms are being played? Are they mostly eighth notes or sixteenth notes? Usually, the more technique players have, the more they employ complex rhythms involving syncopations and subdivisions of the beat. The tempo also has a large bearing on the types of rhythms present. Usually, the slower the tempo, the more complex the rhythms are. Lastly, examine the phrasing. Are the phases short or long? Do they typically begin and end on certain beats, or are they varied and unpredictable?

Obviously, one can spend a great deal of time analyzing all of these aspects of a solo and continually discover new things not noticed previously.

FIND LICKS AND LEARN THEM IN TWELVE KEYS

"Stealing" ideas and licks from your favorite players is an essential and effective way to capture their style. This is one of the ways that we develop vocabulary. With much study, a lick can become a natural part of your improvising arsenal. Once many lines and licks have been learned, they can then be endlessly combined and varied to create an entire language. Most great players have utilized this approach. Of course, the hope for every player is eventually to transcend simply "running" one lick into the next and instead, end up with a language that is somewhat derivative but primarily original and unique.

After you have successfully learned and memorized a phrase in twelve keys, try using it on other tunes. Then find another line and repeat the process. Choose lines that aren't too difficult and that you really like the sound of. If this is a new kind of exercise for you, then start by transposing a line that is only one measure long.

PLAY SOLO WITH A PLAY-ALONG ACCOMPANIMENT

Find a backing track or create one and play the transcription along with that. This way, you get to hear how the solo fits with the harmony. By playing without the original soloist, you will be more exposed and can better assess how well you are playing.

CONCLUSION

All of these approaches and techniques are excellent ways to utilize solo transcriptions to their fullest. It is not, however, necessary to do all of them on every transcription you work on. One or more of the approaches, when done diligently, will yield positive results that will permeate every facet of your playing.

THE TRANSCRIPTIONS

Gerald Albright's alto solo on

Against All Odds

(Take a Look At Me Now)
from AGAINST ALL ODDS
from the Phil Collins Big Band *A Hot Night in Paris*

Words and Music by
Phil Collins

2:30

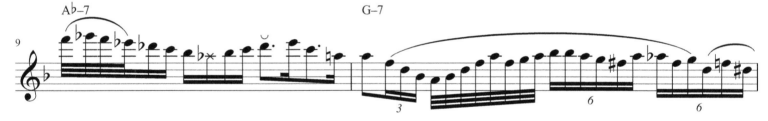

© 1984 EMI GOLDEN TORCH MUSIC CORP. and PHILIP COLLINS LTD.
All Rights except Synchronization Rights Jointly Administered by EMI GOLDEN TORCH MUSIC CORP. and EMI APRIL MUSIC INC. on behalf of PHILIP COLLINS LTD.
Synchronization Rights Exclusively Administered by EMI GOLDEN TORCH MUSIC CORP.
All Rights Reserved   International Copyright Secured   Used by Permission

3

Jay Beckenstein's alto solo on

Morning Dance

from Spyro Gyra's Morning Dance

By Jay Beckenstein

© 1979 Harlem Music, Inc. and Crosseyed Bear Music (BMI)
Administered by Harlem Music, Inc., 1762 Main Street, Buffalo, NY 14208
International Copyright Secured   All Rights Reserved

Michael Brecker's tenor solo on

Still Crazy After All These Years

from Paul Simon's *Still Crazy After All These Years*

Words and Music by
Paul Simon

Copyright © 1974, 1975 Paul Simon (BMI)
International Copyright Secured   All Rights Reserved
Used by Permission

Brandon Fields' alto solo on

I Heard It Through the Grapevine

from *The Traveler*

Words and Music by Norman J. Whitfield
and Barrett Strong

2:55

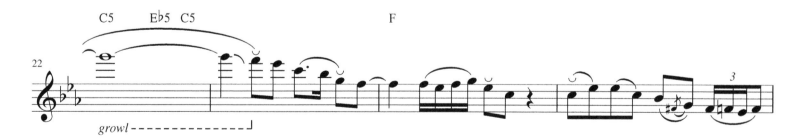

© 1966 (Renewed 1994) JOBETE MUSIC CO., INC.
All Rights Controlled and Administered by EMI BLACKWOOD MUSIC INC. on behalf of STONE AGATE MUSIC (A Division of JOBETE MUSIC CO., INC.)
All Rights Reserved   International Copyright Secured   Used by Permission

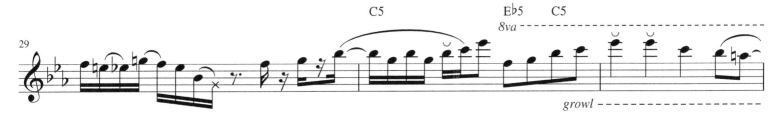

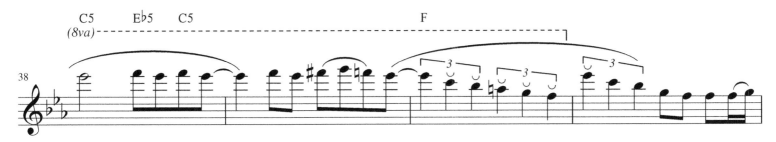

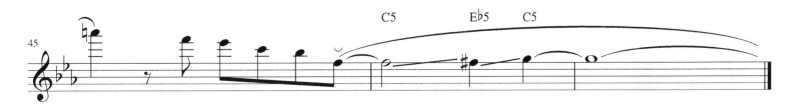

Kenny G's tenor solo on

Midnight Motion

from *Duotones*

Part 1

By Kenny G

1:37

♩ = 110
Swing feel 16th notes

© 1986 EMI BLACKWOOD MUSIC INC., KUZU MUSIC, KENNY G MUSIC and HIGH TECH MUSIC
All Rights for KUZU MUSIC Controlled and Administered by EMI BLACKWOOD MUSIC INC.
All Rights for KENNY G MUSIC Controlled and Administered by UNIVERSAL MUSIC - CAREERS
All Rights Reserved   International Copyright Secured   Used by Permission

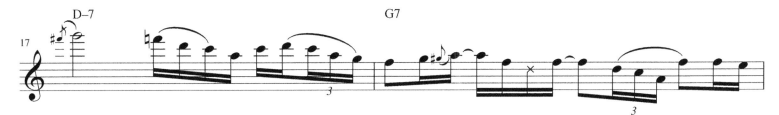

Part 2

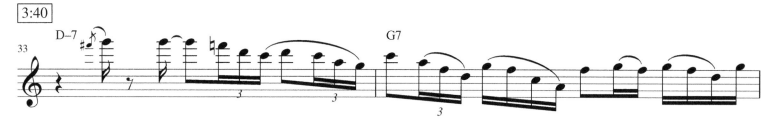

Warren Hill's alto solo on

Baby, I Love Your Way

from Big Mountain's *Unity*

Words and Music by
Peter Frampton

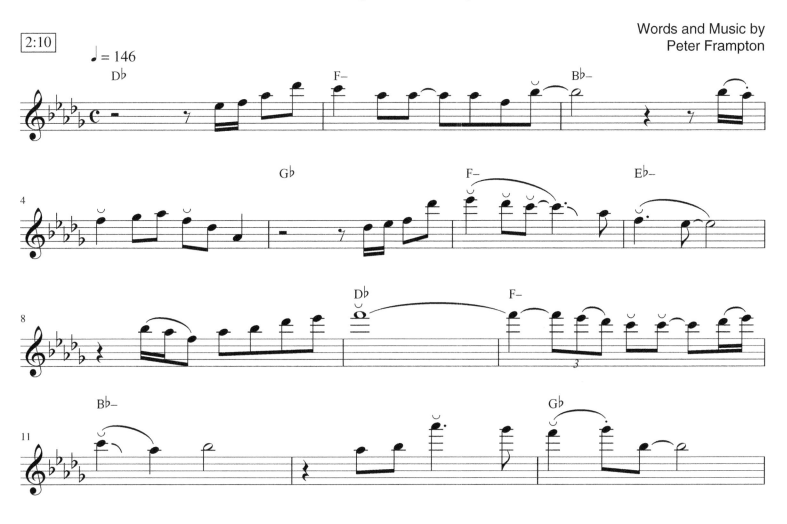

Copyright © 1975 ALMO MUSIC CORP. and NUAGES ARTISTS MUSIC LTD.
Copyright Renewed
All Rights Controlled and Administered by ALMO MUSIC CORP.
All Rights Reserved   Used by Permission

Phil Kenzie's alto solo on

Time Passages

from Al Stewart's *Time Passages*

Part 1

Words and Music by Al Stewart
and Peter White

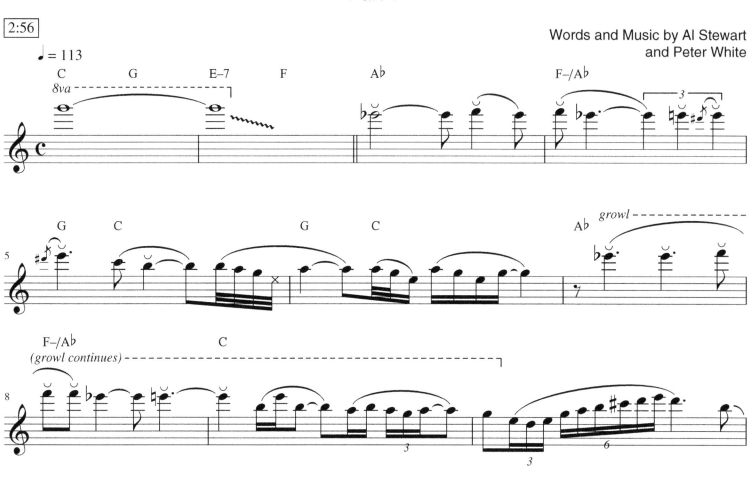

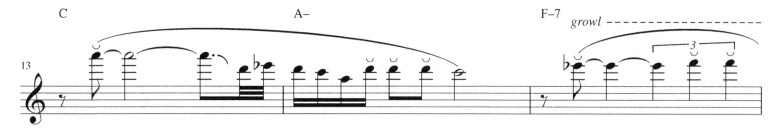

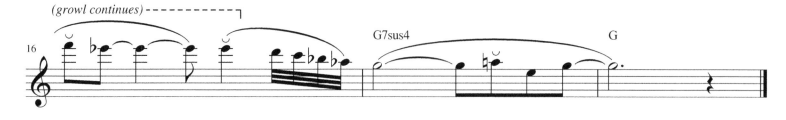

Copyright © 1978 UNIVERSAL/DICK JAMES MUSIC LTD., FRABJOUS MUSIC and APPROXIMATE MUSIC
All Rights for UNIVERSAL/DICK JAMES MUSIC LTD. Controlled and Administered in the U.S. and Canada by UNIVERSAL - SONGS OF POLYGRAM INTERNATIONAL, INC.
All Rights Reserved   Used by Permission

5:02

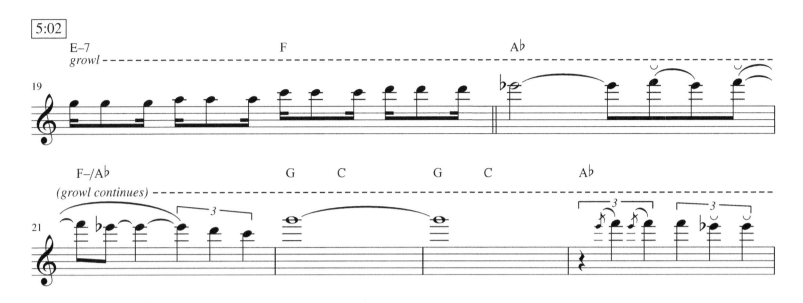

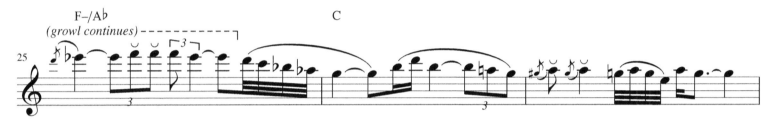

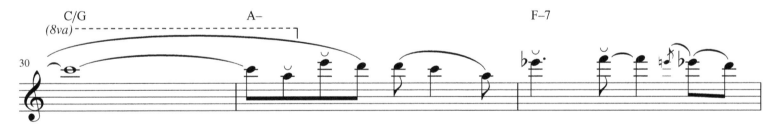

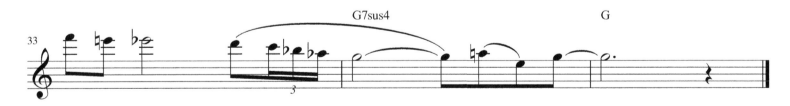

Ray Jarrell's tenor solo on

Stormy

from The Classics IV's *The Very Best of The Classics IV*

Words and Music by J.R. Cobb
and Buddy Buie

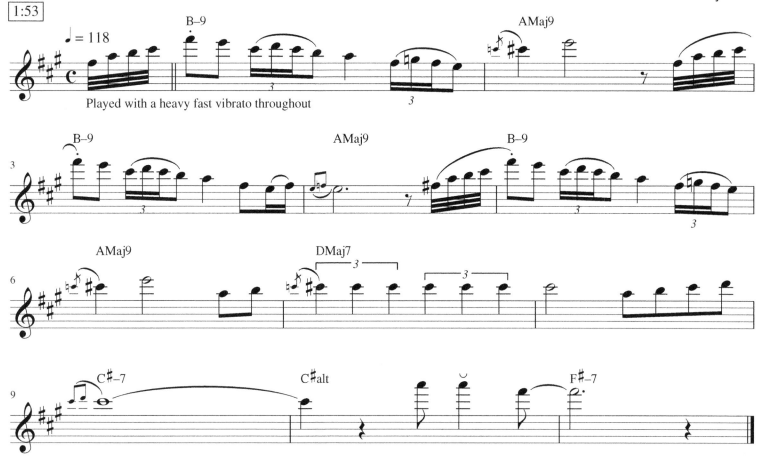

Played with a heavy fast vibrato throughout

Copyright © 1969 Sony/ATV Music Publishing LLC
Copyright Renewed
All Rights Administered by Sony/ATV Music Publishing LLC, 8 Music Square West, Nashville, TN 37203
International Copyright Secured   All Rights Reserved

Ronnie Ross' baritone solo on

Walk on the Wild Side

from Lou Reed's *Transformer*

Words and Music by
Lou Reed

Copyright © 1972 Oakfield Avenue Music Ltd.
Copyright Renewed
All Rights Administered by Spirit One Music
International Copyright Secured   All Rights Reserved

Marc Russo's tenor solo on

Love Is a Wonderful Thing

from Michael Bolton's *Time, Love and Tenderness*

Words and Music by Michael Bolton
and Andy Goldmark

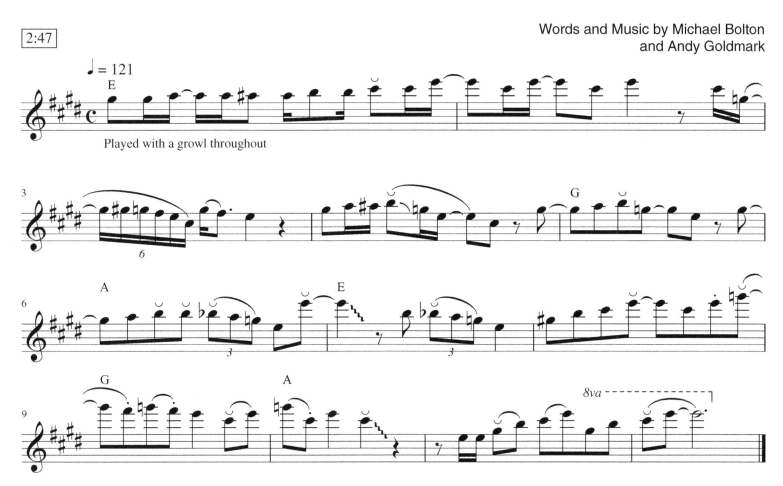

Played with a growl throughout

© 1991 MR. BOLTON'S MUSIC and SHAPIRO, BERNSTEIN & CO., INC.
All Rights for MR. BOLTON'S MUSIC Controlled and Administered by EMI BLACKWOOD MUSIC INC.
All Rights Reserved   International Copyright Secured   Used by Permission

David Sanborn's alto solo on

Ooo Baby Baby

from Linda Ronstadt's *Living in the USA*

Words and Music by William "Smokey" Robinson
and Warren Moore

© 1965, 1972 (Renewed 1993, 2000) JOBETE MUSIC CO., INC.
All Rights Controlled and Administered by EMI APRIL MUSIC INC.
All Rights Reserved   International Copyright Secured   Used by Permission

Clifford Scott's tenor solo on

Honky Tonk

(Parts 1 & 2)

from Bill Doggett's *Leaps and Bounds*

Part 2

Words and Music by Berisford "Shep" Shepherd,
Clifford Scott, Bill Doggett and Billy Butler

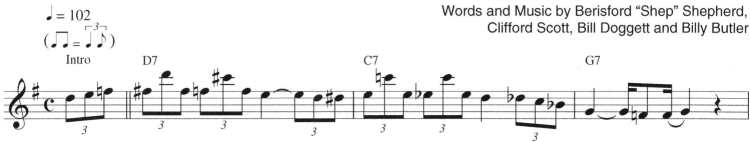

Copyright © 1956 Sony/ATV Music Publishing LLC, Iza Music Corporation, Islip Music and W & K Music
Copyright Renewed
All Rights on behalf of Sony/ATV Music Publishing LLC and Iza Music Corporation Administered by Sony/ATV Music Publishing LLC, 8 Music Square West, Nashville, TN 37203
International Copyright Secured   All Rights Reserved

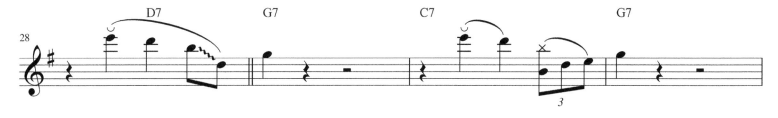

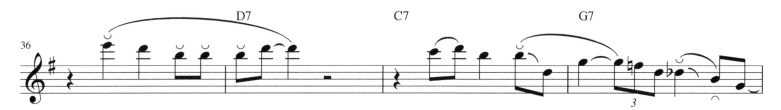

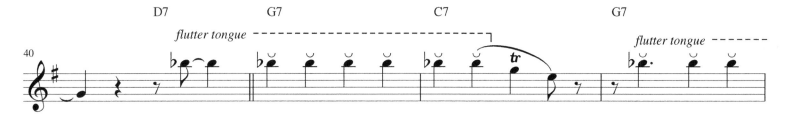

Jay Scott's alto solo on

I Love the Night Life

by Alicia Bridges

Part 1

Words and Music by Alicia Bridges
and Susan Hutcheson

Solo is largely growled

(Solo continues behind vocalist)

Copyright © 1977 Sony/ATV Music Publishing LLC
Copyright Renewed
All Rights Administered by Sony/ATV Music Publishing LLC, 8 Music Square West, Nashville, TN 37203
International Copyright Secured   All Rights Reserved

Part 2

Solo is largely growled

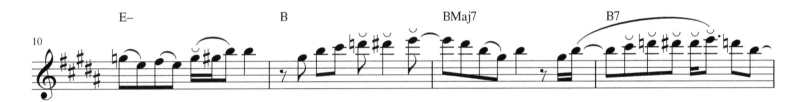

(Solo continues behind vocalist)

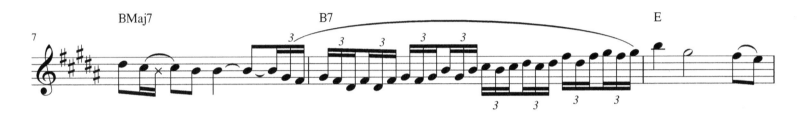

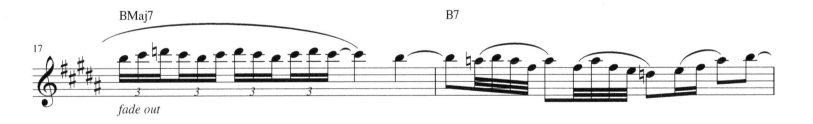

fade out

V. Jeffrey Smith's tenor solo on

Get Outta My Dreams, Get Into My Car

by Billy Ocean from *Tear Down These Walls*

Words and Music by Billy Ocean
and R.J. Lange

Played with a steady growl throughout entire solo

Copyright © 1988 by Aqua Music Ltd. and Out Of Pocket Productions Ltd.
All Rights in the world Administered by Universal Music Publishing International Ltd.
All Rights in the United States Administered by Universal Music - Z Tunes LLC
International Copyright Secured   All Rights Reserved

Don Wilkerson's tenor solo on

Hallelujah I Love Her So

from Ray Charles' *Hallelujah I Love Her So*

Words and Music by
Ray Charles

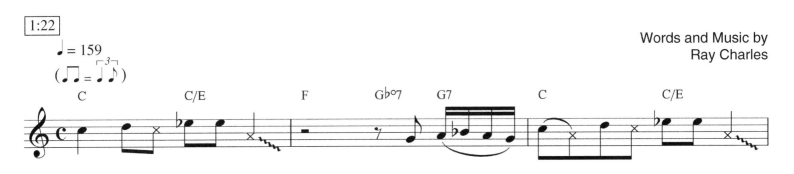

Copyright © 1956 by Unichappell Music Inc.
Copyright Renewed
International Copyright Secured   All Rights Reserved

Junior Walker's tenor solo on

What Does It Take
(To Win Your Love)
by Jr. Walker & The All Stars

Words and Music by John Bristol,
Vernon Bullock and Harvey Fuqua

© 1968 (Renewed 1996) JOBETE MUSIC CO., INC.
All Rights Controlled and Administered by EMI APRIL MUSIC INC. and EMI BLACKWOOD MUSIC INC.
on behalf of JOBETE MUSIC CO., INC. and STONE AGATE MUSIC (A Division of JOBETE MUSIC CO., INC.)
All Rights Reserved   International Copyright Secured   Used by Permission

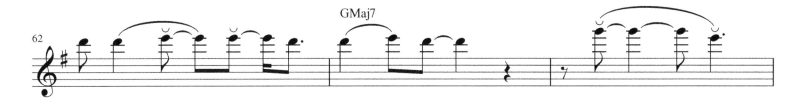

fade out

Phil Woods' alto cadenza on

Have a Good Time

from Paul Simon's *Still Crazy After All These Years*

Words and Music by
Paul Simon

Copyright © 1975 (Renewed) Paul Simon (BMI)
International Copyright Secured   All Rights Reserved
Reprinted by Permission of Music Sales Corporation

About the Author

Saxophonist Jeff Harrington is a professor at Berklee College of Music, a Massachusetts Institute of Technology Affiliated Artist, and a Harvard University MLSP Instructor.

An active performer, he has performed in Europe, St. Thomas, the Philippines, Barbados, Los Angeles, Martinique, the southwest United States, and throughout New England.

His recordings include *Cosmic Motion Picture* as a leader, *One* by the Reed Dieffenbach Quartet, and *Home Cookin'* (Reed Dieffenbach Sextet), among others.

His other books include *Blues Improvisation Complete* (Berklee Press), *Essential Solos on Standard Progressions* (Advance), *Great Tenor Saxophone Solos, Vol. 1 & 2* (Oasis Press), *Great Smooth Jazz, R&B, and Pop Tenor Saxophone Solos* (Oasis Press), and *Written Solos on Standard Tunes* (Oasis Press).

Through his *International Online Jazz Lessons*, he distance-teaches improvisation and saxophone worldwide.

Please visit his website at http://jeffharrington.com/.

More Fine Publications

Berklee Press

GUITAR

BERKLEE ESSENTIAL GUITAR SONGBOOK
Kim Perlak, Sheryl Bailey, and Members of the Berklee Guitar Department Faculty
00350814 Book......................................$22.99

BERKLEE GUITAR CHORD DICTIONARY
Rick Peckham
50449546 Jazz - Book.........................$14.99
50449596 Rock - Book.........................$12.99

BERKLEE GUITAR STYLE STUDIES
Jim Kelly
00200377 Book/Online Media...........$24.99

BERKLEE GUITAR THEORY
Kim Perlak and Members of the Berklee Guitar Department Faculty
00276326 Book......................................$24.99

BLUES GUITAR TECHNIQUE
Michael Williams
50449623 Book/Online Audio...........$29.99

CLASSICAL TECHNIQUE FOR THE MODERN GUITARIST
Kim Perlak
00148781 Book/Online Audio..............$19.99

COUNTRY GUITAR STYLES
Mike Ihde
00254157 Book/Online Audio............$24.99

CREATIVE CHORDAL HARMONY FOR GUITAR
Mick Goodrick and Tim Miller
50449613 Book/Online Audio............$22.99

FUNK/R&B GUITAR
Thaddeus Hogarth
50449569 Book/Online Audio............$19.99

GUITAR SWEEP PICKING
Joe Stump
00151223 Book/Online Audio..............$19.99

JAZZ GUITAR FRETBOARD NAVIGATION
Mark White
00154107 Book/Online Audio.............$22.99

MODAL VOICINGS FOR GUITAR
Rick Peckham
00151227 Book/Online Media.............$24.99

A MODERN METHOD FOR GUITAR – VOLUMES 1-3 COMPLETE*
William Leavitt
00292990 Book/Online Media..........$49.99
Individual volumes, media options, and supporting songbooks available.

A MODERN METHOD FOR GUITAR SCALES
Larry Baione
00199318 Book...$14.99

TRIADS FOR THE IMPROVISING GUITARIST
Jane Miller
00284857 Book/Online Audio...........$22.99

BASS

BERKLEE JAZZ BASS
Rich Appleman, Whit Browne & Bruce Gertz
50449636 Book/Online Audio...........$22.99

CHORD STUDIES FOR ELECTRIC BASS
Rich Appleman & Joseph Viola
50449750 Book.......................................$17.99

FINGERSTYLE FUNK BASS LINES
Joe Santerre
50449542 Book/Online Audio...........$24.99

FUNK BASS FILLS
Anthony Vitti
50449608 Book/Online Audio..........$22.99

INSTANT BASS
Danny Morris
50449502 Book/CD...............................$9.99

METAL BASS LINES
David Marvuglio
00122465 Book/Online Audio.............$19.99

READING CONTEMPORARY ELECTRIC BASS
Rich Appleman
50449770 Book......................................$22.99

PIANO/KEYBOARD

BERKLEE JAZZ KEYBOARD HARMONY
Suzanna Sifter
00138874 Book/Online Audio............$29.99

BERKLEE JAZZ PIANO
Ray Santisi
50448047 Book/Online Audio..........$22.99

BERKLEE JAZZ STANDARDS FOR SOLO PIANO
Robert Christopherson, Hey Rim Jeon, Ross Ramsay, Tim Ray
00160482 Book/Online Audio...........$22.99

CHORD-SCALE IMPROVISATION FOR KEYBOARD
Ross Ramsay
50449597 Book/CD...............................$19.99

CONTEMPORARY PIANO TECHNIQUE
Stephany Tiernan
50449545 Book/DVD...........................$39.99

HAMMOND ORGAN COMPLETE
Dave Limina
00237801 Book/Online Audio............$24.99

JAZZ PIANO COMPING
Suzanne Davis
50449614 Book/Online Audio............$22.99

LATIN JAZZ PIANO IMPROVISATION
Rebecca Cline
50449649 Book/Online Audio.........$29.99

PIANO ESSENTIALS
Ross Ramsay
50448046 Book/Online Audio..........$26.99

SOLO JAZZ PIANO
Neil Olmstead
50449641 Book/Online Audio............$42.99

DRUMS

BEGINNING DJEMBE
Michael Markus & Joe Galeota
00148210 Book/Online Video..............$16.99

BERKLEE JAZZ DRUMS
Casey Scheuerell
50449612 Book/Online Audio............$26.99

DRUM SET WARM-UPS
Rod Morgenstein
50449465 Book......................................$15.99

A MANUAL FOR THE MODERN DRUMMER
Alan Dawson & Don DeMichael
50449560 Book......................................$14.99

MASTERING THE ART OF BRUSHES
Jon Hazilla
50449459 Book/Online Audio............$19.99

PHRASING
Russ Gold
00120209 Book/Online Media............$19.99

WORLD JAZZ DRUMMING
Mark Walker
50449568 Book/CD..............................$27.99

BERKLEE PRACTICE METHOD

GET YOUR BAND TOGETHER
With additional volumes for other instruments, plus a teacher's guide.
Bass
Rich Appleman, John Repucci and the Berklee Faculty
50449427 Book/CD..............................$24.99
Drum Set
Ron Savage, Casey Scheuerell and the Berklee Faculty
50449429 Book/CD...............................$17.99
Guitar
Larry Baione and the Berklee Faculty
50449426 Book/CD...............................$19.99
Keyboard
Russell Hoffmann, Paul Schmeling and the Berklee Faculty
50449428 Book/Online Audio............$19.99

VOICE

BELTING
Jeannie Gagné
00124984 Book/Online Media............$22.99

THE CONTEMPORARY SINGER
Anne Peckham
50449595 Book/Online Audio...........$29.99

JAZZ VOCAL IMPROVISATION
Mili Bermejo
00159290 Book/Online Audio.............$19.99

TIPS FOR SINGERS
Carolyn Wilkins
50449557 Book/CD...............................$19.95

VOCAL WORKOUTS FOR THE CONTEMPORARY SINGER
Anne Peckham
50448044 Book/Online Audio..........$27.99

YOUR SINGING VOICE
Jeannie Gagné
50449619 Book/Online Audio............$29.99

Berklee Press publications feature material developed at Berklee College of Music.
To browse the complete Berklee Press Catalog, go to
www.berkleepress.com

WOODWINDS & BRASS

TRUMPET SOUND EFFECTS
Craig Pederson & Ueli Dörig
00121626 Book/Online Audio.............$14.99

SAXOPHONE SOUND EFFECTS
Ueli Dörig
50449628 Book/Online Audio...........$17.99

THE TECHNIQUE OF THE FLUTE
Joseph Viola
00214012 Book...........................$19.99

STRINGS/ROOTS MUSIC

BERKLEE HARP
Felice Pomeranz
00144263 Book/Online Audio...........$24.99

BEYOND BLUEGRASS BANJO
Dave Hollander and Matt Glaser
50449610 Book/CD.......................$19.99

BEYOND BLUEGRASS MANDOLIN
John McGann and Matt Glaser
50449609 Book/CD.......................$19.99

BLUEGRASS FIDDLE & BEYOND
Matt Glaser
50449602 Book/CD.......................$19.99

CONTEMPORARY CELLO ETUDES
Mike Block
00159292 Book/Online Audio...........$24.99

EXPLORING CLASSICAL MANDOLIN
August Watters
00125040 Book/Online Media..........$24.99

THE IRISH CELLO BOOK
Liz Davis Maxfield
50449652 Book/Online Audio..........$27.99

JAZZ UKULELE
Abe Lagrimas, Jr.
00121624 Book/Online Audio...........$24.99

MUSIC THEORY & EAR TRAINING

BEGINNING EAR TRAINING
Gilson Schachnik
50449548 Book/Online Audio...........$17.99

BERKLEE CONTEMPORARY MUSIC NOTATION
Jonathan Feist
00202547 Book...........................$24.99

BERKLEE MUSIC THEORY
Paul Schmeling
50449615 Book 1/Online Audio........$27.99
50449616 Book 2/Online Audio.......$24.99

CONTEMPORARY COUNTERPOINT
Beth Denisch
00147050 Book/Online Audio..........$24.99

MUSIC NOTATION
Mark McGrain
50449399 Book...........................$27.99
Matthew Nicholl & Richard Grudzinski
50449540 Book...........................$24.99

REHARMONIZATION TECHNIQUES
Randy Felts
50449496 Book...........................$29.99

CONDUCTING

CONDUCTING MUSIC TODAY
Bruce Hangen
00237719 Book/Online Media...........$24.99

MUSIC PRODUCTION & ENGINEERING

AUDIO MASTERING
Jonathan Wyner
50449581 Book/CD.......................$34.99

AUDIO POST PRODUCTION
Mark Cross
50449627 Book...........................$27.99

CREATING COMMERCIAL MUSIC
Peter Bell
00278535 Book/Online Media..........$19.99

HIP-HOP PRODUCTION
Prince Charles Alexander
50449582 Book/Online Audio..........$24.99

THE SINGER-SONGWRITER'S GUIDE TO RECORDING IN THE HOME STUDIO
Shane Adams
00148211 Book...........................$19.99

UNDERSTANDING AUDIO
Daniel M. Thompson
00148197 Book...........................$44.99

MUSIC BUSINESS

CROWDFUNDING FOR MUSICIANS
Laser Malena-Webber
00285092 Book...........................$17.99

ENGAGING THE CONCERT AUDIENCE
David Wallace
00244532 Book/Online Media...........$16.99

HOW TO GET A JOB IN THE MUSIC INDUSTRY
Keith Hatschek with Breanne Beseda
00130699 Book...........................$27.99

MAKING MUSIC MAKE MONEY
Eric Beall
00355740 Book...........................$29.99

MUSIC INDUSTRY FORMS
Jonathan Feist
00121814 Book...........................$17.99

MUSIC LAW IN THE DIGITAL AGE
Allen Bargfrede
00366048 Book...........................$24.99

MUSIC MARKETING
Mike King
50449588 Book...........................$24.99

PROJECT MANAGEMENT FOR MUSICIANS
Jonathan Feist
50449659 Book...........................$39.99

THE SELF-PROMOTING MUSICIAN
Peter Spellman
00119607 Book...........................$29.99

ARRANGING & IMPROVISATION

ARRANGING FOR HORNS
Jerry Gates
00121625 Book/Online Audio...........$24.99

BERKLEE BOOK OF JAZZ HARMONY
Joe Mulholland & Tom Hojnacki
00113755 Book/Online Audio...........$29.99

MODERN JAZZ VOICINGS
Ted Pease and Ken Pullig
50449485 Book/Online Audio..........$27.99

Prices subject to change without notice. Visit your local music dealer or bookstore, or go to **www.berkleepress.com**

SONGWRITING/COMPOSING

BEGINNING SONGWRITING
Andrea Stolpe with Jan Stolpe
00138503 Book/Online Audio...........$22.99

COMPLETE GUIDE TO FILM SCORING
Richard Davis
50449607 Book...........................$34.99

THE CRAFT OF SONGWRITING
Scarlet Keys
00159283 Book/Online Audio...........$24.99

CREATIVE STRATEGIES IN FILM SCORING
Ben Newhouse
00242911 Book/Online Media...........$27.99

JAZZ COMPOSITION
Ted Pease
50448000 Book/Online Audio $39.99

MELODY IN SONGWRITING
Jack Perricone
50449419 Book...........................$26.99

MUSIC COMPOSITION FOR FILM AND TELEVISION
Lalo Schifrin
50449604 Book...........................$39.99

POPULAR LYRIC WRITING
Andrea Stolpe
50449553 Book...........................$17.99

THE SONGWRITER'S WORKSHOP
Jimmy Kachulis
Harmony
50449519 Book/Online Audio $29.99
Melody
50449518 Book/Online Audio $24.99

SONGWRITING: ESSENTIAL GUIDE
Pat Pattison
Lyric Form and Structure
50481582 Book...........................$19.99
Rhyming
00124366 Book...........................$22.99

SONGWRITING IN PRACTICE
Mark Simos
00244545 Book...........................$16.99

SONGWRITING STRATEGIES
Mark Simos
50449621 Book...........................$27.99

SONGBOOKS

NEW STANDARDS
Terri Lyne Carrington
00369515 Book...........................$29.99

WELLNESS/AUTOBIOGRAPHY

LEARNING TO LISTEN: THE JAZZ JOURNEY OF GARY BURTON
Gary Burton
00117798 Book...........................$34.99

MANAGE YOUR STRESS AND PAIN THROUGH MUSIC
Dr. Suzanne B. Hanser and Dr. Susan E. Mandel
50449592 Book/Online Audio $34.99

MUSICIAN'S YOGA
Mia Olson
50449587 Book...........................$19.99

NEW MUSIC THERAPIST'S HANDBOOK
Dr. Suzanne B. Hanser
00279325 Book...........................$32.99

LEARN MUSIC ONLINE WITH BERKLEE

Berklee college of music

Study Berklee College of Music's renowned curriculum directly from our faculty. Improve your skills in all areas of music with:

 Bachelor of Professional Studies Online Degree

 Multi-Course Certificate Programs

In-Depth, Highly Interactive Online Courses

online.berklee.edu

1-866-BERKLEE (USA) | +1-617-747-2146 (INTL)

■ **BERKLEE ONLINE**

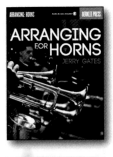

Berklee Press

Your Source for Composing, Arranging & Conducting

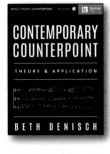

ARRANGING FOR HORNS
by Jerry Gates
00121625 Book/Online Audio $22.99

ARRANGING FOR LARGE JAZZ ENSEMBLE
by Dick Lowell and Ken Pullig
50449528 Book/Online Audio $39.99

ARRANGING FOR STRINGS
by Mimi Rabson
00190207 Book/Online Audio $22.99

THE BERKLEE BOOK OF JAZZ HARMONY
by Joe Mulholland & Tom Hojnacki
00113755 Book/Online Audio $29.99

BERKLEE CONTEMPORARY MUSIC NOTATION
by Jonathan Feist
00202547 Book $24.99

BERKLEE MUSIC THEORY
by Paul Schmeling
Book 1: Basic Principles of Rhythm, Scales and Intervals
50449615 Book/Online Audio $24.99
Book 2: Fundamentals of Harmony
50449616 Book/Online Audio $24.99

COMPLETE GUIDE TO FILM SCORING
The Art and Business of Writing Music for Movies and TV
by Richard Davis
50449607 Book $34.99

CONDUCTING MUSIC TODAY
by Bruce Hangen
00237719 Book/Online Video $24.99

CONTEMPORARY COUNTERPOINT
Theory & Application
by Beth Denisch
00147050 Book/Online Audio $24.99

COUNTERPOINT IN JAZZ ARRANGING
by Bob Pilkington
00294301 Book/Online Audio $24.99

CREATING COMMERCIAL MUSIC
Advertising • Library Music • TV Themes
by Peter Bell
00278535 Book/Online Media $19.99

CREATIVE STRATEGIES IN FILM SCORING
by Ben Newhouse
00242911 Book/Online Media $27.99

JAZZ COMPOSITION
Theory and Practice
by Ted Pease
50448000 Book/Online Audio $39.99

JAZZ EXPRESSION
A Toolbox for Improvisation
with Larry Monroe
50448036 DVD $19.95

MODERN JAZZ VOICINGS
Arranging for Small and Medium Ensembles
by Ted Pease and Ken Pullig
50449485 Book/Online Audio $24.99

MUSIC COMPOSITION FOR FILM AND TELEVISION
by Lalo Schifrin
50449604 Book $39.99

MUSIC NOTATION
Theory & Technique for Music Notation
by Mark McGrain
50449399 Book $24.99

MUSIC NOTATION
Preparing Scores and Parts
by Matthew Nicholl and Richard Grudzinski
50449540 Book $24.99

REHARMONIZATION TECHNIQUES
by Randy Felts
50449496 Book $29.99

Berklee Press publications feature material developed at Berklee College of Music.

Visit your local music dealer or bookstore to order, or go to www.berkleepress.com

Prices, contents, and availability subject to change without notice.

Berklee Online

Earn a Bachelor's Degree Online for 60% Less Than Campus Tuition

Berklee Online's Bachelor of Professional Studies degree program is the most affordable and flexible option for earning a degree from Berklee College of Music.

- Earn Experiential Credit for Previous Industry Experience

- Transfer Credits Accepted from Accredited Institutions

- Federal Financial Aid Available

Apply Now for an Online Degree in:

Music Production • Music Business • Music Composition for Film, TV & Games
Interdisciplinary Music Studies • Electronic Music Production & Sound Design
Songwriting • and more

online.berklee.edu

1-866-BERKLEE (USA) | +1-617-747-2146 (INTL)

🐦 @BerkleeOnline
f /BerkleeOnline
▶ /BerkleeMusic